MAPPING
THE AMERICAN
PROMISE

Historical Geography Workbook
Volume II from 1865

MARK NEWMAN
University of Illinois, Chicago

Bedford Books 〰 Boston

For information, write: Bedford Books,
75 Arlington Street, Boston MA 02116 (617–426–7440)

ISBN 0–312–18242–2

PREFACE

Though historians disagree on many things, consensus exists on one important issue: We study and teach change over time and space. Not surprisingly, history has not been immune to the forces of change. The discipline is in the midst of a deep-rooted and substantial reform movement that is well known to history teachers. In teaching, the trend is toward a more student-centered model that uses a variety of interactive methods. The idea is to directly involve students in the learning process and thus enable them to acquire the knowledge, understanding, and skills they need to succeed in college and life.

In recent years, publishers have contributed to history education reform by expanding textbook coverage of different peoples and including special sections that allow more in-depth exploration of relevant topics. They have also surrounded the textbooks with an array of ancillaries that extend learning by helping instructors better engage their students in interactive exercises. Those old, familiar resources, maps, have assumed greater importance because they are such versatile tools. They not only supply a spatial context for content, showing who did what, where and when, but help students develop important skills needed to study history effectively. Also, students like maps.

Mapping The American Promise offers a novel approach to the use of maps in history instruction. The sixty-four workbook exercises explore maps included in the text on three levels: reading the map, connecting the information in the map to content in the chapter, and exploring the map to extend learning. Some activities show students how to manage large amounts of diverse information by having them organize data into tables, charts, timelines, or chronologies. Some place students in historical situations and ask them to make decisions, while others can be used to engender lively discussion in the classroom. An answer key is available so you or the student can check the work.

My hope is that this map workbook will stimulate student interest in history and increase student knowledge and understanding of the historical process by developing skills in reading and note taking, observation and visual analysis, critical thinking and managing information, and writing. To paraphrase the motto of an old television show, American history and maps have many tales to tell, here are sixty-four of the best.

A NOTE TO THE STUDENT

Maps and textbooks. For most of your education, maps and textbooks have been familiar resources. Many of your classrooms were adorned with maps that brightened up the decor and also helped locate the nations and peoples you studied. In virtually every subject, textbooks have been your primary source of information. So a natural connection exists between maps and texts. Maps graphically depict who did what, when, and where, thus supplying the necessary context in which to place the textbook content. In other words, maps help organize information so you can make sense of it. The goals of *Mapping The American Promise* are to build upon this integral relationship and to enable you to use maps with your textbook to enhance your knowledge and understanding of history as well as to stimulate your interest in the subject.

The need to organize and make sense of information is part and parcel of a history education. The goal of studying history is not just to know dates and names—far from it; instead, the idea is to have you study a wide range of facts to analyze their meaning and significance. History strives not just for knowledge, but for understanding. We identify the who, what, how, when, and where of history to figure out the why. History helps explain who we are and how we got here, and offers insight into where we are going.

Maps are important aids in this quest for knowledge and understanding—and have been used in education since antiquity. Inscribed on a clay tablet, the oldest world map is from ancient Babylonia. With other clay tablets that served as the textbooks, the map was used in Babylonian schools to teach children who they were and where they lived in the universe.

Today, maps perform a similar function and much more, because the nature of education has changed. In the past, a major difficulty was a relative lack of readily available information. Today, computers and the Internet, the vast publishing industry, and the media have created a different problem. We are daily bombarded with so much information that it's hard to make sense of everything being thrown at us. Mastering the enormous content of a college history survey class often seems overwhelming. I am sure you recognize that studying history in college requires you to perform at a higher level than in high school in terms of reading, thinking, and writing.

There are two keys to mastering the large amounts of information you encounter in a college history class. One is developing your reading, note-taking, critical thinking, and writing skills so that you select pertinent data, analyze it effectively, and then write your conclusion in a clear, succinct manner. The other is placing the data in a context that facilitates understanding. It is one thing to know about something and another to understand it. History stresses gaining knowledge for understanding.

Maps help you learn history by supplying a visual image that takes in the larger picture of the topic under study. Maps graphically depict a vast amount of diverse information in a variety of ways. By supplying a spatial context to the historical process in a single image, they help you see both the big picture and the important details of various trends and events. But as is true for history generally, you must ask the right questions to open the fruitful dialogue with a map that yields knowledge and understanding.

The sixty-four exercises in *Mapping The American Promise*—two per chapter—directly connect to the content of the text. Generally, they have a three-part format. "Reading the Map" asks you to identify pertinent information on the map. "Connecting to the Chapter" links the map content and context to relevant information in the text chapter. "Exploring the Map" extends the dialogue in numerous and often creative ways, perhaps linking map content to primary sources or the historical question of the chapter, referring to content from past chapters, or challenging you to make decisions about historical events by placing you in the situation depicted on the map.

Other exercises offer different activities related to managing information and developing thinking skills. Constructing a timeline or chronology will help you place historical content in the correct time context. Developing charts and tables teaches you how to organize, categorize, and analyze large amounts of diverse information.

Most journeys require a map to get to the destination. So as you open this workbook and begin your trek through history, use the maps wisely to enjoy your travels and to reach your destination a more intelligent and more competent person than when you began. Good luck!

CONTENTS

MAPPING
THE AMERICAN
PROMISE

CHAPTER 16

RECONSTRUCTION
1863–1877

Introduction

The end of slavery destroyed the foundations of the South's plantation economy. The conditions of the immediate postwar years strongly influenced the rise of a new system based on farm tenancy, and while many things changed, much remained the same for planters and African Americans. See *The American Promise,* page 631.

READING THE MAP

1. Compare and contrast the southern plantation in 1861 and 1881. What remained the same and what changed?

_____

_____

_____

_____

_____

_____

_____

_____

_____

2. Looking at the changes in the layout and structure of the plantations, determine what the freed African Americans gained.

_____

_____

_____

_____

_____

_____

_____

_____

_____

_____

_____

CONNECTING TO THE CHAPTER

Developing a new system of labor and production required accommodating the needs and desires of both planters and African American farmers. Complete the table to compare and contrast their respective needs and desires. Use the boldface entries as a model. Then answer the questions following the table.

	Planters	*African American Farmers*
Landownership		
Labor system		
Personal freedom	**Maintain tight control over African Americans: have them remain in clustered houses and limit their personal freedom**	

MAP 16.1 A Southern Plantation in 1861 and 1881

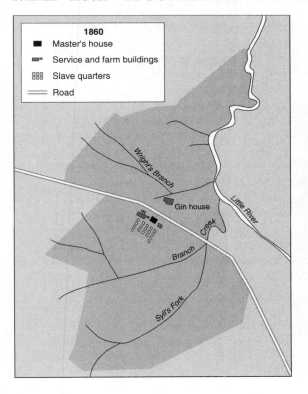
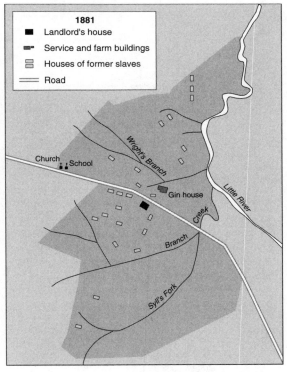

1. In attempting to accommodate the varying needs of planters and labor, what system arose? What prior development influenced its rise?

_____

_____

_____

_____

_____

_____

_____

_____

2. What does it appear that each side gained in the new agricultural system that emerged?

_____

_____

_____

_____

_____

_____

_____

_____

_____

_____

_____

_____

_____

_____

_____

EXPLORING THE MAP

1. From the perspective first of an African American farmer and then of a planter, write two contracts for labor on a southern cotton plantation during Reconstruction. Include specific provisions regarding working conditions and tasks, housing and living conditions, personal freedom and family rights, and payment. Compare a real sharecropping contract to yours. Which of your contracts—African American or planter—is closer to the real one? What does this tell you about power in the South during Reconstruction?

_____

_____

_____

_____

_____

_____

_____

_____

_____

_____

_____

_____

_____

_____

_____

_____

_____

NOTES

RECONSTRUCTION
1863–1877

Introduction

Various groups had differing ideas on how to reconstruct the South. The interplay between these ideas and the programs developed often makes understanding reconstruction difficult. While Map 16.3 contains much information on where reconstruction occurred and when important events happened, this information is just the tip of the iceberg—nine-tenths of the reconstruction story remains hidden. See *The American Promise*, page 636.

PUTTING RECONSTRUCTION IN PERSPECTIVE

1. Using Map 16.3, list in chronological order the readmission of former states to the Union. Then list in chronological order the reestablishment of conservative governments.

MAP 16.3   *The Reconstruction of the South*

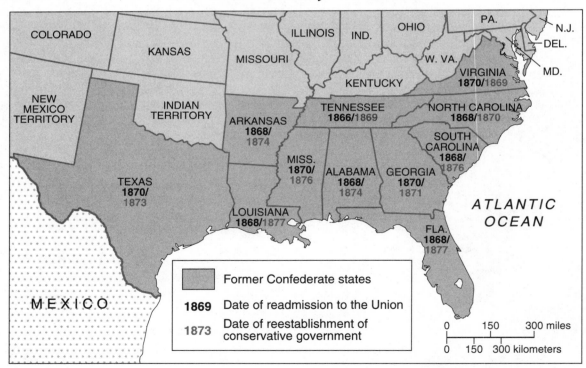

Five Issues	1. The status and treatment of Confederate government officials and military
	2.
	3.
	4.
	5.

Three Reconstruction Programs	1. Lincoln: Swift readmission for national unity. After 10% of the qualified voters in 1860 renounced secession and slavery, state reconstructed.
	2.
	3.

Acts and Constitutional Amendments	1. December 1863: Proclamation of Amnesty and Reconstruction (Lincoln plan)
	2. July 1864:
	3. March 1865:
	4. Fall 1865:
	5. December 1865:
	6. April 1866:
	7. June 1866:
	8. July 1866:
	9. March 1867:
	10. February 1869:

(Question 1 continues) _____

_____

_____

_____

_____

_____

_____

2. Complete the above table, using the bold-face entries as models. Then answer the questions after the table to examine the various Reconstruction programs.

3. What issue did none of the plans address? Why?

_____

_____

_____

4. From the point of view of a white planter or an African American politician/farmer in the South in 1867, write an editorial that critiques the congressional Reconstruction program and offers changes in that program, including provisions for the issue not addressed by the various plans.

5. Assess how well the U.S. Reconstruction program worked. Did it "reconstruct" the nation? Explain your answer.

NOTES

CHAPTER 17

AMERICANS ON THE MOVE: THE SETTLEMENT OF THE WEST AND THE RISE OF THE CITY
1860–1900

Introduction

The last four decades of the nineteenth century can rightly be called the age of the railroad. The phenomenal spread of the rail lines throughout the United States was greatly aided by federal and state land grants. See *The American Promise,* page 648.

READING THE MAP

1. Locate the major east–west railroad routes. Identify these routes by name, endpoints, and whether or not they were land grants. Include only routes passing through several states.

2. Which states had the most rail lines running through them? Were land grants used on these routes?

3. What other type of transportation is prominent on the map? What were the names of these routes and where did they go? Do you notice anything about their locations that might relate to railroad construction?

CONNECTING TO THE CHAPTER

1. How much land did the railroads receive as grants, and how much did this land increase in value?

_____

_____

_____

2. What was the general impact of the railroads on national development?

_____

_____

_____

MAP 17.1 Federal Land Grants to Railroads and the Development of the West, 1850–1900

3. What impact did the railroads have on Native Americans?

_____

_____

_____

_____

_____

EXPLORING THE MAP

1. On a separate piece of paper, design a promotional brochure for a railroad company that will be sent to the residents of a western town that might be on the route of the rail line. The time period is the late 1860s or 1870s. In the brochure, describe the benefits the railroad will bring to the town and what the town might lose if the railroad goes elsewhere.

NOTES

AMERICANS ON THE MOVE: THE SETTLEMENT OF THE WEST AND THE RISE OF THE CITY

1860–1900

Introduction

A continuing theme of the nineteenth century was westward movement and settlement. This expansion of the United States had tragic consequences for Native Americans, who lost most of their lands. The period between 1850 and 1890 was characterized by warfare between Native Americans and the United States. The result was the decimation of native peoples not only through armed conflict but also through the devastating effects of government policies and practices that eliminated the groups' traditional means of livelihood. See *The American Promise*, page 661.

READING THE MAP

1. Though Native Americans lived throughout the West, not all states and territories experienced warfare. In what states and territories did the major battles occur? From the map, determine which peoples offered the greatest violent resistance to white encroachment.

2. What was the first conflict and what was the last? What Native American peoples were involved in both battles?

3. One of the most famous battles was Custer's Last Stand. Identify that battle, won by the Sioux over Custer in 1876.

CONNECTING TO THE CHAPTER

1. In total, what was the change in Native American population in the area that became the United States between 1492 and 1890?

2. The United States pursued three policies toward Native Americans. What were these policies? What were their goals? What were their results?

(Question 2 continues)

MAP 17.3 *The Loss of Indian Lands, 1850–1890*

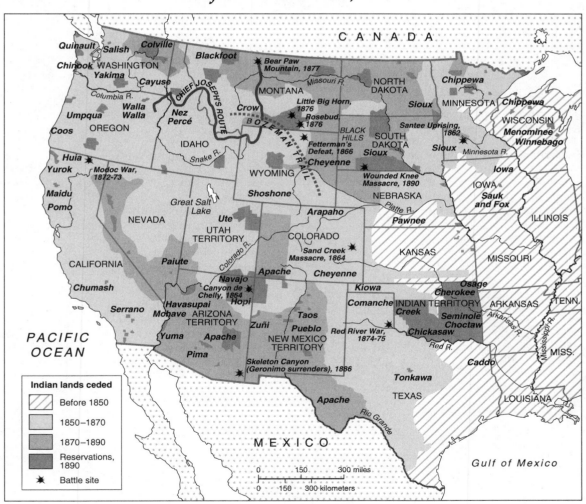

3. The massacre at Wounded Knee ended Native American resistance and closed a chapter in Native American history. What was the movement that precipitated the events leading to the massacre and what happened at Wounded Knee?

Exploring the Map

1. Using the U.S. Bill of Rights as a guide, write a bill of rights for Native Americans.

2. Write a newspaper editorial on the Wounded Knee massacre that assesses the danger posed by the Ghost Dance religion, the actions of the army at Wounded Knee, and the impact of the massacre on the Sioux.

NOTES

CHAPTER 18

BUSINESS AND POLITICS IN THE GILDED AGE
1877–1895

Introduction

A major theme in U.S. history covered in several previous exercises was the spread of transportation. The development of transportation proceeded in phases, often determined by advances in technology. The use of navigable rivers and Native American trails was followed by the building of roads and canals. But it was not until the railroad that a fast, effective means of crossing long distances over land was available. The period from 1870 to 1890 witnessed a flurry of railroad construction that not only connected the Pacific coast and western cities to the East but also allowed isolated rural areas access to the rest of the nation. See *The American Promise,* page 692.

READING THE MAP

1. Before 1879, where were most of the railroad lines located? What were the endpoints of the only western route?

_____

_____

_____

_____

_____

_____

2. Compare Map 18.1 with Map 17.1, which shows railroad land grants. On what routes in the West were land grants largely used? Where were they not used? The federal government provided most of the grants. Refer to your answer for question 1 under "Reading the Map" for Map 17.1, and identify the government's goal in providing land to railroad companies.

_____

_____

_____

_____

_____

_____

_____

3. What were the major railroad centers in the Midwest and South?

_____

_____

_____

_____

_____

CONNECTING TO THE CHAPTER

1. The chapter suggests that railroads had a huge effect on the nation's economy.

Complete the following chart to show how the railroad affected various aspects of economic development. Then answer the question following the chart.

Economic development	Effects of railroads
Market development	
Business development	**Stimulated rise of steel industry** **Made innovations in food processing and meatpacking possible**
Urban development	

MAP 18.1   Railroad Expansion, 1870–1890

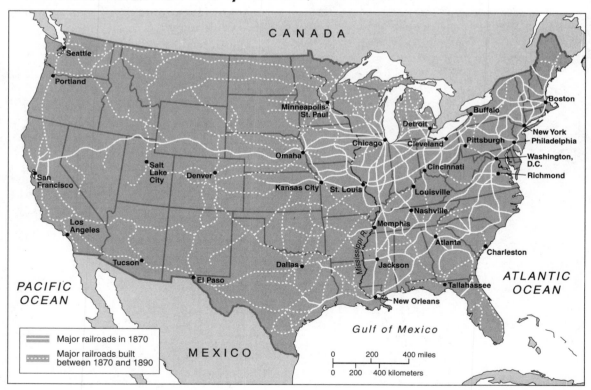

2. According to chapter 18, the construction of railroads proceeded under less than optimal conditions. What conditions characterized rail line construction? How do these conditions fit within the definition of the Gilded Age?

EXPLORING THE MAP

1. A familiar sight along rail lines was the telegraph. Why was the telegraph so important to rail travel?

2. The time zones were created by the railroad companies. Plan a trip from Chicago through Omaha to San Francisco and return from San Francisco to Los Angeles and then to Chicago via Tucson, El Paso, Dallas, and St. Louis. Assume that no time zones exist. What problems would you encounter? How would time zones overcome these difficulties?

NOTES

BUSINESS AND POLITICS IN THE GILDED AGE
1877–1895

Introduction

The Gilded Age witnessed many political changes as the emergence of political bosses and corruption tarnished the nation's political fabric and gave rise to various reform movements. The 1884 presidential election began as a classic confrontation between those involved in machine party politics and reformers dedicated to eliminating corruption from government, but it quickly degenerated into a vicious, mudslinging campaign. See *The American Promise*, page 715.

READING THE MAP

1. Where were the Democratic and Republican areas of strength? Assess the election results and determine which party seemed stronger and which party won. Why do you think that party's candidate won?

2. How many states did Blaine win and how many did Cleveland win? Given the number of states won by each candidate, why was the vote so close?

3. How did the respective strengths of the Democrats and Republicans reflect Civil War and Reconstruction divisions? How did Cleveland overcome these divisions?

CONNECTING TO THE CHAPTER

1. Construct profiles of Blaine and Cleveland
   to highlight their differences.

MAP 18.2   The Election of 1884

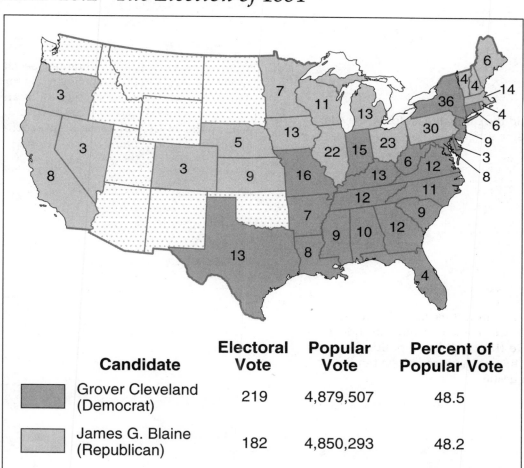

Candidate	Electoral Vote	Popular Vote	Percent of Popular Vote
Grover Cleveland (Democrat)	219	4,879,507	48.5
James G. Blaine (Republican)	182	4,850,293	48.2

2. Both candidates suffered from mudslinging. What bombshell rocked Cleveland's candidacy, and what incident may have cost Blaine the election?

_____

_____

_____

_____

_____

_____

_____

_____

_____

_____

3. How did the campaign styles of Cleveland and Blaine differ?

_____

_____

_____

_____

_____

EXPLORING THE MAP

1. Write an editorial backing the presidency of either Cleveland or Blaine. Include testimony to the candidate's political careers and to the incidents mentioned in the previous questions.

_____

_____

_____

_____

_____

_____

_____

_____

_____

2. Write a sensationalist, mudslinging speech for either Cleveland or Blaine. If writing for Blaine, attack Cleveland's fathering of an illegitimate child. If writing for Cleveland, focus on the incident in which Blaine alienated Irish Catholic voters.

_____

_____

_____

_____

_____

_____

_____

_____

_____

_____

_____

NOTES

CHAPTER 19

AMERICA THROUGH THE EYES OF THE WORKERS
1870–1890

Introduction

The period between 1865 and 1900 witnessed the rise of the United States as an industrial power. This rise was strongly connected to geography and had profound implications on jobs and occupations, tasks, and workplaces. See *The American Promise*, page 726.

GEOGRAPHY, RESOURCES, AND INDUSTRY

Complete the following table, listing the resources and industries for each region, to make connections between geography and industrialization. Use the boldface entries as models. Then answer the questions after the table. The regions are defined as follows.

Northeast: Maryland through Maine, Atlantic through Pennsylvania.

South: Gulf Coast to Ohio River, Texas to Atlantic.

Midwest: North of Ohio River to Canada, Missouri-Iowa-Minnesota western border through Ohio.

West: All other states.

	Resources	Industries
Northeast	**Coal**	**Food and beverage processing**
South		
Midwest		
West		

1. Which regions had the most diverse economies?

_____

_____

2. Which region had no industry but was vital to industrialization because of its resources?

_____

_____

3. What type of industry crossed the most regional boundaries? What does this indicate

about the United States' potential as an industrial nation?

_____

_____

_____

_____

_____

MAP 19.1 *Industrialization, 1865–1900*

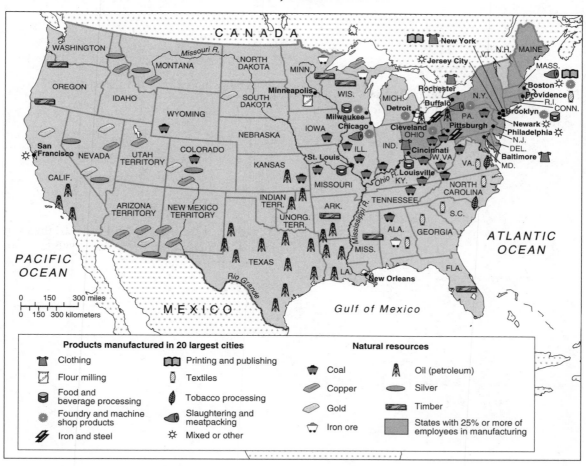

Products manufactured in 20 largest cities

Clothing	Printing and publishing
Flour milling	Textiles
Food and beverage processing	Tobacco processing
Foundry and machine shop products	Slaughtering and meatpacking
Iron and steel	Mixed or other

Natural resources

Coal	Oil (petroleum)
Copper	Silver
Gold	Timber
Iron ore	States with 25% or more of employees in manufacturing

4. What resources and industries were located in your state? What are the major industries in your state today? Has the industrial situation in your state changed? If it has, how has it changed?

_____

_____

_____

_____

_____

_____

_____

5. How does this map on industrialization fit the depiction of economic regions in Map 19.2?

_____

_____

_____

_____

_____

_____

_____

_____

INDUSTRY AND WORK

1. Industrialization transformed virtually every facet of work, but many people still held jobs in traditional, pre-industrial occupations. According to chapter 19, what industries employed the following types of workers?

   a. Common laborer (pick and shovel)

   _____

   b. Skilled worker

   _____

   c. Factory operative

   _____

   d. Sweatshop worker

   _____

2. What was the new managerial class?

   _____

   _____

   _____

   _____

3. How did technology and industrialization aid women in the workplace? Where were the gains evident?

   _____

   _____

   _____

   _____

NOTES

AMERICA THROUGH THE EYES OF THE WORKERS
1870–1890

Introduction

The industrial revolution divided the world into distinct, hierarchical economic regions. To a great extent, a nation's progress and power in the world community depended on industrializing its economy. The modern economic distinctions among nations first became evident in the nineteenth century, and they continue to divide the world today. See *The American Promise,* page 728.

READING THE MAP

1. We are used to dividing the world into the West and the East, but Map 19.2 provides a different geographic division of three economic regions. What are these regions and where are they located?

   _____

   _____

   _____

2. What areas of the world were not part of any of the three regions, and how would you characterize these areas?

   _____

   _____

   _____

3. Where did the United States fit in this economic division? What does that characterization say about its stage of development in the late nineteenth century?

   _____

   _____

   _____

   _____

CONNECTING TO THE CHAPTER

1. According to chapter 19, what were the geographic bounds of the three economic regions?

   _____

   _____

   _____

   _____

   _____

   _____

   _____

   _____

   _____

2. What was the relationship of the three regions?

_____

_____

_____

_____

_____

_____

_____

3. How did the role played by the rural agricultural regions as a supplier of labor affect the United States?

_____

_____

_____

_____

_____

_____

_____

MAP 19.2 *Economic Regions of the World*

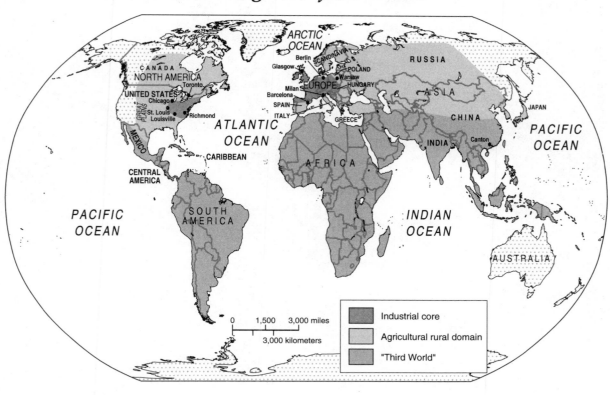

EXPLORING THE MAP

1. What bias is evident in Map 19.2 from the division of the world into three regions?

_____

_____

_____

_____

_____

_____

_____

_____

2. How would a map of economic regions today compare with this one? What similarities would exist? What differences?

_____

_____

_____

_____

_____

_____

_____

_____

_____

NOTES

FIGHTING FOR CHANGE IN THE TURBULENT NINETIES
1890–1900

Introduction

In the last decades of the nineteenth century, U.S. foreign policy changed greatly and became much more important. See *The American Promise*, page 784.

PUTTING U.S. FOREIGN POLICY IN PERSPECTIVE

To help place U.S. foreign policy in perspective, use Map 20.3 and chapter 20 to complete the chart below. Use the boldface entries as models. Then answer the questions following the chart.

Americas	Eastern Hemisphere

1. Keep Americas closed to outside influences

Influences

Policies

1. Open Door

1. Pan-American cooperation for hemispheric peace and trade

1. Missionary Activity

Initiatives

Results

1. How did the United States divide the world? How did this division affect foreign policy?

_____

_____

_____

_____

_____

_____

_____

_____

_____

_____

2. Where was U.S. expansion headed, and why?

_____

_____

_____

_____

_____

_____

_____

_____

_____

_____

_____

MAP 20.3   U.S. Territorial Expansion through 1900

3. Using both economic and democratic needs, write a foreign policy statement for or against U.S. imperialism.

NOTES

FIGHTING FOR CHANGE IN THE TURBULENT NINETIES

1890–1900

Introduction

The Spanish-American War was a turning point in the age of imperialism and U.S. history. The United States replaced Spain as an imperial power and faced the task of administering an overseas empire of subject peoples while espousing a doctrine of democracy. See *The American Promise,* page 791.

READING THE MAP

1. How did the geography of the arenas of the Spanish-American war influence how it was fought and won?

    _____

    _____

    _____

    _____

    _____

    _____

2. What tactic used by the United States navy in the Civil War was employed with good results in the Spanish-American War?

    _____

    _____

    _____

3. Naval battles were pivotal to the U.S. victory. What were these naval battles? Where and when were they fought?

    _____

    _____

    _____

    _____

    _____

    _____

4. U.S. forces also won three important land battles on the same day. What were these battles, where were they fought, and on what day?

    _____

    _____

    _____

    _____

    _____

    _____

CONNECTING TO THE CHAPTER

1. Though Americans expressed genuine concern over the plight of Cubans rebelling against Spain, the road to war was paved by newspaper chains fighting over circulation. Whose newspaper chains helped pre-

cipitate the war? What type of journalism
did they employ, and what tragedy did
they exploit that led to war?

_____

_____

_____

_____

MAP 20.4   *The Spanish-American War, 1898*

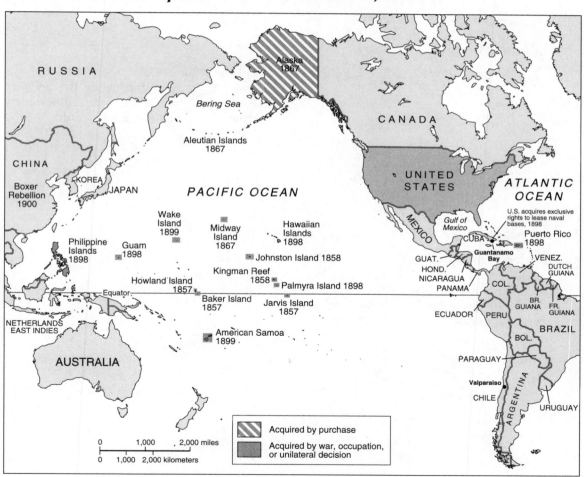

2. Theodore Roosevelt played an important role in the Spanish-American War. How and in what capacities before and during the war did he contribute to an American victory?

_____

_____

_____

_____

_____

3. Who called the American conflict with Spain that "Splendid Little War"? Why was it "splendid"?

_____

_____

_____

_____

_____

EXPLORING THE MAP

1. Write a newspaper editorial opposing the Spanish-American War and the acquisition of former Spanish colonies. Attack the war effort on the grounds of democratic rights, liberty, and the use of yellow journalism.

_____

_____

_____

_____

2. For the soldiers fighting in Cuba, the war was hardly splendid. Using the primary sources in Chapter 20, write a diary entry from the perspective of a soldier who fought at San Juan Hill.

_____

_____

_____

_____

_____

_____

_____

_____

NOTES

CHAPTER 21

PROGRESSIVE REFORM FROM THE GRASSROOTS TO THE WHITE HOUSE
1890–1916

Introduction

The progressive movement touched virtually every aspect of American society. One of the more enduring reforms was the conservation efforts that led to the establishment of national parks and forests. See *The American Promise*, page 819.

READING THE MAP

1. Where are most of the national parks and forests located? Why do you think they are concentrated in this region?

   _____

   _____

   _____

2. How many national parks are there? In what states are national parks located? Which states have the most parks? How many do these states have?

   _____

   _____

   _____

   _____

   _____

   _____

3. What were the first and last national parks established? Where are they, and when were they founded?

   _____

   _____

   _____

   _____

   _____

   _____

CONNECTING TO THE CHAPTER

1. Theodore Roosevelt played a major role in the conservation movement. How many acres of government land reserves existed when he took office? How many acres did he add to the reserves? How many national monuments, wildlife refuges, and national parks did he establish?

   _____

   _____

   _____

   _____

   _____

2. What forces fought the conservation movement?

_____

_____

_____

_____

_____

_____

_____

_____

_____

3. Who was Roosevelt's main government ally and how did they block the efforts of conservation opponents?

_____

_____

_____

_____

_____

_____

_____

_____

_____

MAP 21.1   *National Parks and Forests*

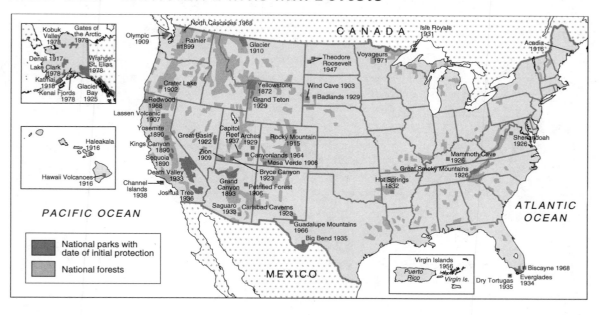

EXPLORING THE MAP

1. Have you ever visited a national park? Which one? What impressed you the most? If you have not visited a national park, which one would you like to see and why?

NOTES

PROGRESSIVE REFORM FROM THE GRASSROOTS TO THE WHITE HOUSE
1890–1916

Introduction

Having coasts on two oceans separated by a three-thousand-mile-wide continent created transportation difficulties that posed military and economic problems for the United States. The railroad helped alleviate land transport dilemmas, while the Panama Canal greatly reduced the distance by sea from New York to San Francisco. See *The American Promise,* page 822.

READING THE MAP

1. How long was the trip from New York to San Francisco before the Panama Canal? How long was it after the canal was built? Approximately what percentage of the distance was cut by building the canal?

2. Why was Panama a likely site for a canal?

3. What two cities served as the ports for the Panama Canal?

4. Looking at the map, try to determine where construction proved most difficult, and why.

CONNECTING TO THE CHAPTER

1. Why did Theodore Roosevelt want a canal?

2. Two sites for the canal were proposed. What site besides Panama was suggested? Which site seemed more likely for a canal, and why? What determined the selection of Panama?

3. How did Roosevelt's desire for a canal lead
   to independence for Panama?

_____   _____

_____   _____

_____   _____

_____   _____

_____   _____

MAP 21.2   *The Panama Canal, 1914*

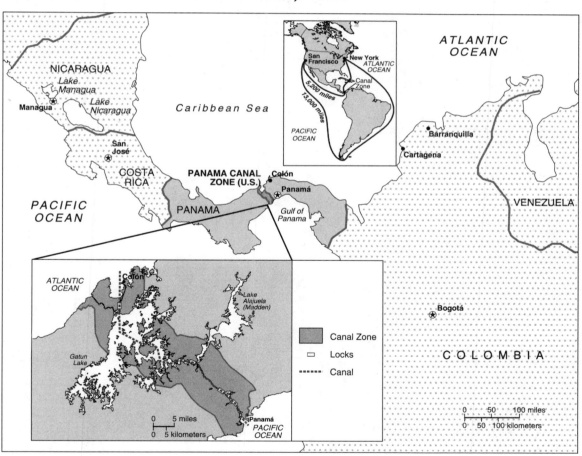

EXPLORING THE MAP

1. The Panama Canal was not the only important canal built before World War I to eliminate the need to sail around a continent. What other canal was built during this period that eliminated travel around what continent?

_____

_____

_____

_____

_____

_____

_____

_____

_____

_____

_____

_____

_____

_____

_____

_____

_____

_____

_____

_____

_____

2. The rugged terrain in Panama made building the canal arduous, long, and dangerous. Research the construction of the Panama Canal to find out how long it took to build, who the workers were, and what conditions they labored under. Record your findings.

_____

_____

_____

_____

_____

_____

_____

_____

_____

_____

_____

_____

_____

_____

_____

_____

_____

_____

_____

_____

_____

NOTES

CHAPTER 22

THE UNITED STATES AND THE "GREAT WAR"
1914–1920

Introduction

World War I pitted two alliances of primarily European nations against each other in four brutal years of warfare. Ironically, the rulers of several of the opposing nations were relatives, so the war, from one perspective, was a very tragic family quarrel. See *The American Promise*, page 850.

READING THE MAP

1. To get a sense of who was involved in World War I, identify the nations constituting the Central Powers, the Allied Powers, and neutral countries.

2. How did the geography of the alliances favor the Allied Powers?

3. Where did the events leading to World War I start? What significance does this place have today?

CONNECTING TO THE CHAPTER

1. The wartime alliances grew out of prewar combinations. What were these prewar combinations, and who belonged to each? How did the prewar alliance structure affect the coming of war? Were any changes made in the alliances after war broke out?

2. To show how the alliance system contributed to war, describe the course of events that led to the outbreak of hostilities.

_____ _____

_____ _____

_____ _____

_____ _____

_____ _____

_____ _____

MAP 22.2 *European Alliances after the Outbreak of World War I*

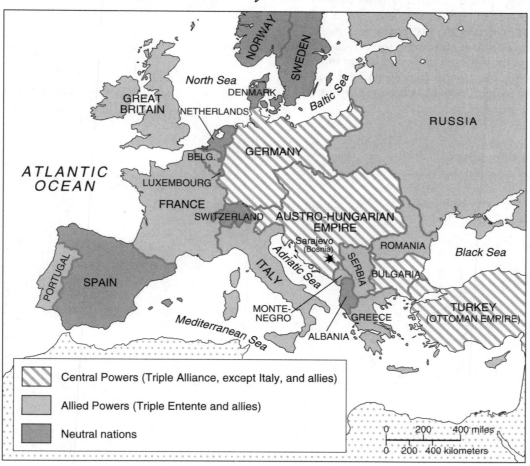

3. Why was the "Great War" a world war?

_____

_____

_____

_____

_____

_____

_____

EXPLORING THE MAP

1. The recent breakup of Yugoslavia and the resulting armed conflict in the Balkans raised fears of another major war over this region. Referring to newspaper and magazine accounts, explain why the recent violence in the Balkans did not escalate into a major war. Could similar steps have prevented World War I? Why, or why not?

NOTES

THE UNITED STATES AND THE "GREAT WAR"
1914–1920

Introduction

The Nineteenth Amendment guaranteed women the right to vote. Before its passage in 1920, however, many states had already granted women suffrage. See *The American Promise,* page 858.

READING THE MAP

1. Does Map 22.3 show a geographic theme to woman suffrage? If so, what was it and what were its characteristics?

_____

_____

_____

2. What was the first state to grant women the right to vote, and when? Was this place a state when women gained the vote? How many states extended the vote to women during the World War I years (1914–1918)? What were they, and what were the dates when women began voting?

_____

_____

_____

_____

_____

3. What does this map indicate about the strategy used by women's rights groups to gain the vote?

_____

_____

CONNECTING TO THE CHAPTER

1. The fight for woman suffrage encountered fierce resistance and defeat in several states. Describe the actions taken in New York in 1915 and Ohio in 1917 and the outcomes.

_____

_____

_____

_____

_____

_____

_____

_____

_____

_____

_____

2. During World War I, suffragists redirected their focus. What did they concentrate on during the war? What strategies did they use, and what was the outcome?

_____

_____

_____

_____

_____

_____

3. The Nineteenth Amendment required passage by two-thirds of the states for ratification. Looking at the map and the events in New York and Ohio, do you think that the amendment was or was not likely to pass, and why?

_____

_____

_____

_____

_____

MAP 22.3   Women's Voting Rights before the Nineteenth Amendment

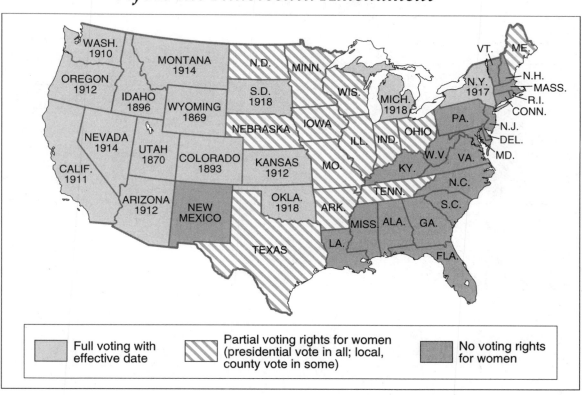

Full voting with effective date	Partial voting rights for women (presidential vote in all; local, county vote in some)	No voting rights for women

EXPLORING THE MAP

1. Using the experience of women in World War I, write a newspaper editorial supporting women's right to vote.

_____

_____

_____

_____

_____

_____

_____

_____

_____

_____

_____

_____

_____

_____

_____

_____

_____

_____

_____

_____

_____

_____

_____

_____

_____

2. Why do you think western states were the first to give women the right to vote?

_____

_____

_____

_____

_____

_____

_____

_____

_____

_____

_____

_____

_____

_____

_____

_____

_____

_____

_____

_____

_____

_____

_____

_____

_____

NOTES

CHAPTER 23

FROM "NORMALCY" TO THE GREAT DEPRESSION
1920–1932

Introduction

The election of 1920 returned the presidency to the Republicans after eight years of Democratic rule. The triumph of Warren G. Harding signaled a change in the mood of many Americans who sought less turbulent times. See *The American Promise,* page 890.

READING THE MAP

1. Warren G. Harding's 1920 victory was the biggest landslide in presidential elections up to that time. How many states did he carry? Was his victory a national mandate, that is, did he have strong support from all sections of the country? Why, or why not?

2. What southern state turned its back on tradition and voted for Harding?

3. What candidate received no electoral votes? What was his party, and how many popular votes did he receive?

CONNECTING TO THE CHAPTER

1. The slogan of Harding's campaign was "normalcy." What did he mean by that term?

2. On what issue did Woodrow Wilson try to make the 1920 election a referendum, and how did his actions affect the Democratic Party's fortunes in the presidential election?

3. What were the keys to Harding's success?

MAP 23.1 *The Election of 1920*

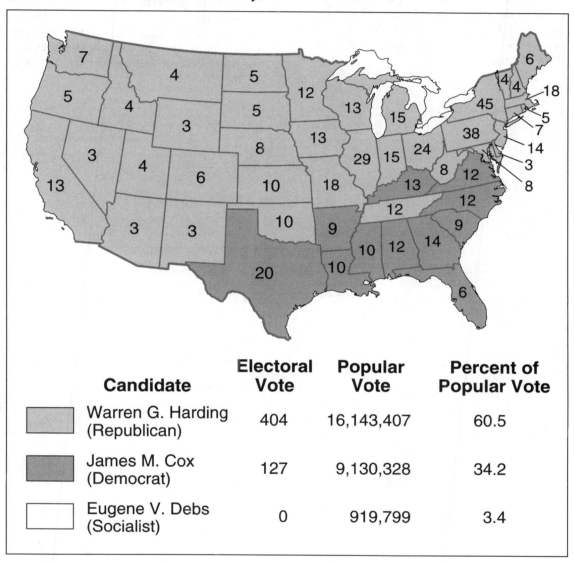

Candidate	Electoral Vote	Popular Vote	Percent of Popular Vote
Warren G. Harding (Republican)	404	16,143,407	60.5
James M. Cox (Democrat)	127	9,130,328	34.2
Eugene V. Debs (Socialist)	0	919,799	3.4

EXPLORING THE MAP

1. The 1920 election introduced a future president to the American people and was the final curtain call for a past radical leader. Who were these leaders, and what positions did they aspire to?

2. In some distressing but familiar ways, Harding's administration represented a return to the government practices of the Gilded Age. Refer to chapter 18 and identify the similarities that existed between the questionable or dishonest politics of those years and the politics of the early 1920s.

NOTES

FROM "NORMALCY" TO THE GREAT DEPRESSION
1920–1932

Introduction

The 1920s witnessed the rise of the automobile as the most popular form of everyday transportation. Its emergence created a ripple effect in the American economy as subsidiary industries arose to service both the production and the use of automobiles. See *The American Promise,* page 897.

READING THE MAP

1. How does Map 23.2 show that the auto industry had achieved national dimensions by 1927? How many states had factories related to auto manufacturing?

_____

_____

_____

_____

2. In what regions was automobile manufacturing concentrated, and where was it least evident?

_____

_____

_____

_____

_____

3. Though not shown on Map 23.2, the integration of the automobile into American life depended on strong expansion of what related industry?

_____

_____

_____

_____

_____

CONNECTING TO THE CHAPTER

1. Why did Detroit, Michigan, become the capital of the auto industry? What advantages did Detroit and the Great Lakes states offer to automobile manufacturers?

_____

_____

_____

_____

_____

2. How many workers had jobs directly or indirectly related to the auto industry in 1927?

_____

_____

_____

_____

3. How did the integration of the automobile into everyday life affect American society?

_____

_____

_____

_____

_____

_____

_____

_____

EXPLORING THE MAP

1. What part does the automobile play in your life? Go through the daily routine of your family, noting where an automobile is necessary. How many activities would your family have to forgo if there was no car available? What other transportation options are available?

_____

_____

_____

_____

MAP 23.2 *Auto Manufacturing*

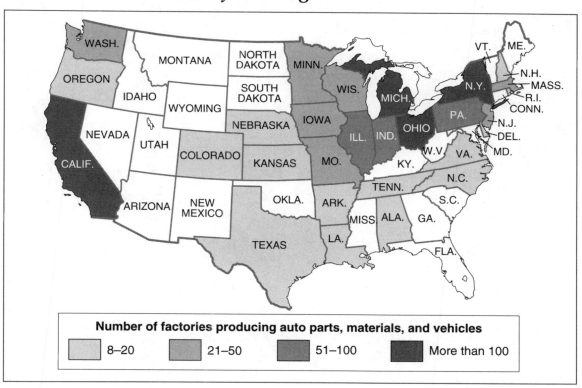

Number of factories producing auto parts, materials, and vehicles

8–20   21–50   51–100   More than 100

(Question 1 continues) _____

_____

_____

_____

_____

_____

_____

_____

_____

_____

_____

_____

_____

_____

_____

_____

_____

_____

_____

_____

_____

_____

_____

_____

_____

_____

2. What other means of transportation—bicycle, bus, railroad, subway, airplane—do you or members of your family use regularly? What are they used for, and how often? Do any of these substitute for the automobile? How? Why?

_____

_____

_____

_____

_____

_____

_____

_____

_____

_____

_____

_____

_____

_____

_____

_____

_____

_____

_____

NOTES

CHAPTER 24

THE NEW DEAL ERA
1932–1939

Introduction

In 1932, for the second time in twelve years, the American people switched party affiliations in presidential contests to create a huge landslide victory. In 1920, the Republicans benefited from this switch, while in 1932, Democratic challenger Franklin Delano Roosevelt was the beneficiary. See *The American Promise*, page 938.

READING THE MAP

1. How many states voted Democratic in 1928? How many states voted Republican in 1932? Calculate how many states shifted from Republican to Democratic between 1928 and 1932.

2. In most elections after the Reconstruction era, southern states voted Democratic. In 1928, however, some southern states went Republican. Which ones?

3. Did any states voting Democratic in 1928 vote Republican in 1932?

CONNECTING TO THE CHAPTER

1. Though the election of 1932 resulted in a landslide victory for Franklin D. Roosevelt, prior to his nomination factions within the party threatened to block his candidacy. Who opposed Roosevelt's candidacy, and why?

2. What moves did Roosevelt make to capture the Democratic nomination?

3. What did Roosevelt's campaign slogans call for, and what past programs did he cite as influences?

_____ _____

_____ _____

_____ _____

_____ _____

_____ _____

_____ _____

_____ _____

MAP 24.2 *Electoral Shift, 1928–1932*

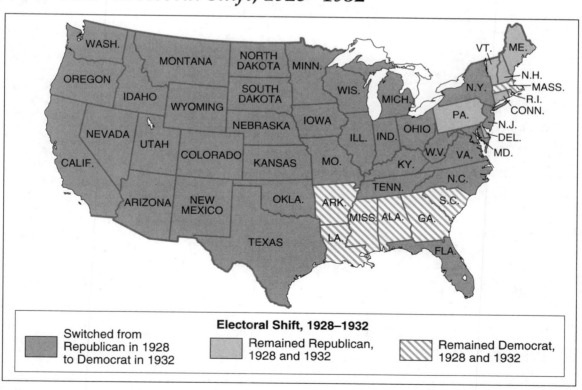

Electoral Shift, 1928–1932

Switched from Republican in 1928 to Democrat in 1932

Remained Republican, 1928 and 1932

Remained Democrat, 1928 and 1932

Exploring the Map

1. Refer to chapters 23 and 24 to write an analysis of landslide victories by comparing and contrasting the 1920 and 1932 presidential elections. Use the following questions as guides. What influenced voters to change parties in each case? What role did the respective personalities of the candidates play in each victory? What issues most animated public opinion, and how did the platforms of the respective candidates address these concerns? Did any other factors influence the landslide victories?

NOTES

THE NEW DEAL ERA
1932–1939

Introduction

One of the major New Deal initiatives was the Tennessee Valley Authority, which involved the federal government in the planned development of a largely poverty-stricken, rural area. See *The American Promise,* page 942.

READING THE MAP

1. Along what river system was the Tennessee Valley Authority established, and what states were involved?

   _____

   _____

   _____

   _____

   _____

2. How many dams and how many power plants were built? In what state were most of these dams and power plants constructed?

   _____

   _____

   _____

   _____

   _____

   _____

   _____

3. What does the building of so many dams suggest about the geography of the Tennessee Valley and the nature of the Tennessee River?

   _____

   _____

   _____

   _____

   _____

CONNECTING TO THE CHAPTER

1. What aim did the TVA fulfill, and what were the goals of the project?

   _____

   _____

   _____

   _____

   _____

   _____

   _____

   _____

   _____

   _____

   _____

   _____

2. How did the TVA try to meets its goals?

_____

_____

_____

_____

_____

_____

3. Who opposed the TVA? What ends did the project realize?

_____

_____

_____

_____

_____

_____

_____

MAP 24.3 *The Tennessee Valley Authority*

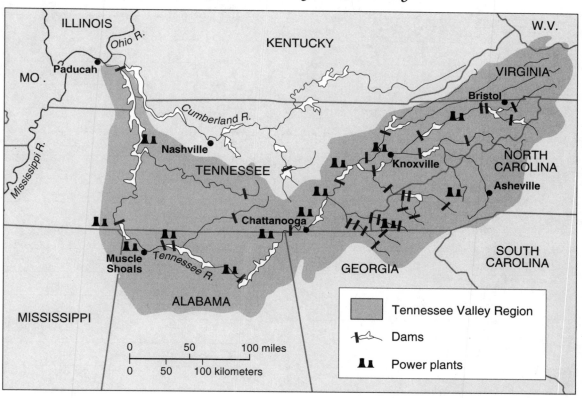

EXPLORING THE MAP

1. Create an inventory of electric power use in your classroom or home. Suppose that electric power was no longer available: How would your education or daily life change? For example, how would you type your papers? How would you illuminate or heat and cool your home? How would you communicate with other people not within the range of your voice? What appliances and technological advances would you have to give up? What alternative power sources would be available?

NOTES

CHAPTER 25

THE UNITED STATES AND THE SECOND WORLD WAR
1939–1945

Introduction

During World War II, Japanese Americans were interned in relocation authority centers. The centers hardly met democratic principles, and those living in them often suffered extreme hardships. See *The American Promise,* page 1002.

READING THE MAP

1. In what states were Japanese Americans most populous?

2. What were the names of the relocation centers, and in what states were they located?

CONNECTING TO THE CHAPTER

1. What was the history of the Japanese in the United States before World War II?

2. How did the military view the Japanese? Why were relocation centers established? Were they justified?

MAP 25.3 *Western Relocation Authority Centers*

Legend:

- WRA relocation camp
- States with more than 1,000 Japanese Americans

EXPLORING THE MAP

1. Referring to the primary source documents on pages 1000–1001 in the textbook, write a diary entry for a Japanese person living in a relocation center.

NOTES

THE UNITED STATES AND THE SECOND WORLD WAR
1939–1945

INTRODUCTION

As in World War I, the United States was a late entry into World War II. But this time the enemies of the United States and its allies — the Axis, composed of Germany and Italy (and Japan in Asia) — controlled most of continental Europe and much of North Africa. An Allied victory thus required a multifront attack strategy. See *The American Promise,* page 1008.

READING THE MAP

1. By 1942, what nations or parts of nations in Europe were under Axis control? What nations had been absorbed before the war?

   _____

   _____

   _____

   _____

   _____

2. What nations remained neutral, and what nations were members of the Allies?

   _____

   _____

   _____

   _____

3. What luxury of war did the United States enjoy, and how did this benefit the Allied cause?

   _____

   _____

   _____

   _____

   _____

   _____

4. The turning point in World War II came in late 1942 and early 1943 when the Allies won three major victories. What were these victories, and when and where were they fought?

   _____

   _____

   _____

   _____

   _____

CONNECTING TO THE CHAPTER

1. The European theater in World War II had three fronts. What were these fronts? When did the Allies initiate actions in each of them? How were Churchill, Stalin, and Roosevelt divided on the timing of the openings of these fronts?

MAP 25.4 *The European Theater of World War II, 1942–1945*

2. D Day was one of the most famous battles in United States history. How long was D Day in the planning? Who headed the Allied and German forces? What handicapped the Germans? How did the Allies fool the Germans?

_____

_____

_____

_____

_____

_____

_____

_____

_____

_____

_____

3. What battle represented the last significant German push? What were its goals, and where and when was it fought? How many German casualties were there, and how did this push affect Germany's chances in the war?

_____

_____

_____

_____

_____

_____

EXPLORING THE MAP

1. World War II was considered a "good war" because of why it was fought. But it also was a devastating conflict. How many people died in World War II? How did deaths compare with military losses? How many Americans died? How many Russians died?

_____

_____

_____

_____

_____

_____

_____

_____

_____

_____

Taking casualties into account, use another piece of paper to write a policy statement proposing a plan for European reconstruction from the perspective of the Soviet Union. In developing this reconstruction plan, keep in mind (a) the number of people killed and what that meant for families and the workforce, (b) coping with the destruction of agricultural fields, factories, hospitals, places of business, and homes, (c) the need to provide health care and rehabilitation for the wounded, (d) the task of raising money to pay for the reconstruction, and (e) the Soviet Union's need for political security after the country had been invaded with disastrous consequences twice in twenty years.

NOTES

CHAPTER 26

COLD WAR POLITICS IN THE TRUMAN YEARS
1945–1953

Introduction

The unity of the Allied war effort unraveled rapidly after the return of peace, and the breakup led to the division of Europe into three camps. See *The American Promise,* page 1025.

READING THE MAP

1. To put the division of Europe into perspective, identify the NATO, Communist bloc, and neutral countries.

2. How did the postwar division of Europe compare with the wartime alliances?

3. How was Berlin divided? Which Allied nation fared best in this division?

CONNECTING TO THE CHAPTER

1. What were the five elements of the U.S. defense strategy in Europe?

2. What is NATO? When was it founded and what is its purpose?

_____

_____

_____

_____

_____

_____

3. What program did the United States institute to help Europe recover from the war and forestall the spread of communism? When did this program begin, and what did it supply?

_____

_____

_____

_____

_____

MAP 26.1   *The Division of Europe after World War II*

EXPLORING THE MAP

1. Using the Soviet Union's experience in World War II and the postwar moves by the United States and its allies as well as those of the Soviet Union, draw a political cartoon that defends or condemns the creation of the iron curtain. If you need help, refer to your daily newspaper for examples of political cartoons.

Notes

COLD WAR POLITICS IN THE TRUMAN YEARS
1945–1953

Introduction

The first military conflict after World War II was in Korea, where the United States and the United Nations attempted to stop the spread of communism. See *The American Promise,* page 1051.

READING THE MAP

1. What type of landform is Korea? What two great Asian powers, one not shown on the map, stand on either side of Korea?

2. Where was Korea divided after World War II?

3. Trace the course of the Korean War. How successful were the offensives launched by both sides initially? What were these offensives, and what did they achieve?

4. Where was the truce line drawn? Did either side gain any territory?

CONNECTING TO THE CHAPTER

1. What led to the division of Korea after World War II?

MAP 26.3   The Korean War, 1950–1953

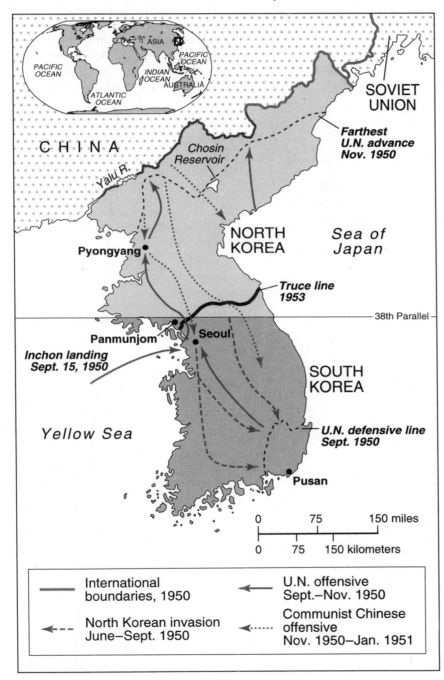

2. How did the United States make the Korean War an international conflict? Why was the Korean War not an official U.S. war?

_____

_____

_____

_____

_____

3. How did President Truman's political policy of containment conflict with General MacArthur's military strategy? How did this conflict affect the conduct of the war and MacArthur's career?

_____

_____

_____

_____

_____

_____

_____

_____

_____

_____

_____

_____

_____

_____

EXPLORING THE MAP

1. The 1952 election revolved around the conduct of the Korean War. Draft a policy statement to end the Korean War either by combat or by diplomacy. Base your statement on either containment or on a strategy of all-out war. Defend your choices.

_____

_____

_____

_____

_____

_____

_____

_____

_____

_____

_____

_____

_____

_____

_____

_____

_____

_____

NOTES

CHAPTER 27

THE POLITICS AND CULTURE OF ABUNDANCE
1952–1960

Introduction

Having witnessed the value of a well-developed, connected highway system in Germany, President Dwight Eisenhower supported a federal program to build an interstate highway system. See *The American Promise*, page 1063.

READING THE MAP

1. In 1930, where were most highways located? Compare Map 27.1 with Map 18.1, which shows railroad expansion. Where did initial railroad development take place?

2. One transcontinental highway route existed in 1930. Where was it, and what borders did it connect?

3. By 1970, the interstate highway system had vastly expanded. Where were most highways located? How many transcontinental routes began in the Pacific coast states? What California city not named on the map was the terminus for most of the transcontinental highways?

CONNECTING TO THE CHAPTER

1. What legislation provided for the construction of the interstate highway system, and when was it enacted?

2. How did the building of highways affect residential trends in the 1950s?

3. How much of the interstate highway system ran through urban areas?

MAP 27.1   *The Interstate Highway System, 1930 and 1970*

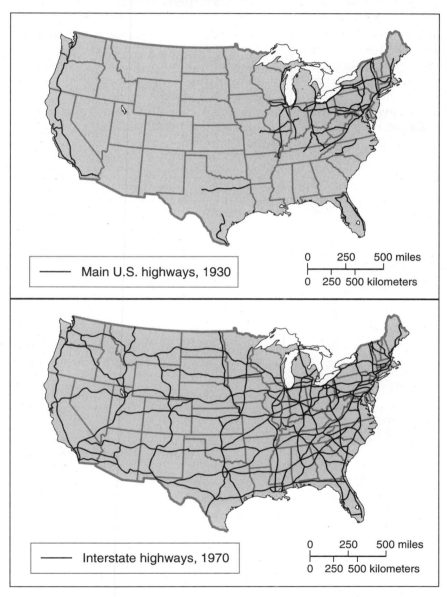

Main U.S. highways, 1930

0   250   500 miles
0   250 500 kilometers

Interstate highways, 1970

0   250   500 miles
0   250 500 kilometers

EXPLORING THE MAP

1. Have you traveled on the interstate highway system? Where did you go, and why? Get a road map and trace your route on the interstate, including destinations and time frames for each day's travel. Then look for alternate routes and trace your trip on these roads. How would your driving experience have differed if there were no interstate? How much longer might it have taken, and what different places might you have visited, if any?

_____

_____

_____

_____

_____

_____

_____

_____

_____

_____

2. Refer to previous maps in the textbook or this workbook that show cattle trails and railroads. Compare the routes taken by the interstate highway system with those of cattle trails and railroads. Did the routes of the earlier transportation routes influence the development of the interstate highway system? Why, or why not? If possible, get a map of the river systems of the United States and assess how the rivers influenced the development of roads, railroads, and highways in the United States.

_____

_____

_____

_____

_____

_____

_____

_____

_____

_____

NOTES

THE POLITICS AND CULTURE OF ABUNDANCE
1952–1960

Introduction

The demography of the nation changed during and after World War II, resulting in much larger populations in the southern tier of the United States, also known as the Sun Belt. See *The American Promise,* page 1079.

READING THE MAP

1. What states experienced the largest growth in population, more than 20 percent increases, between 1940 and 1960? In looking at the states with the greatest growth, can you detect a regional pattern to the rise in population? If so, what was it?

_____

_____

_____

_____

2. What states recorded the highest growth rates, and what were these rates? What states experienced declines in population? How much did their populations decline?

_____

_____

_____

_____

3. What state do you live in? How did its population change between 1940 and 1960? Did your family move into your state during this period? If so, where did your family move from, and why?

_____

_____

_____

_____

_____

_____

_____

_____

_____

_____

_____

_____

CONNECTING TO THE CHAPTER

1. Percentage rates do not always reflect true population growth: A state with a small population can record a high rate of growth through a small influx of people while a

state with a large population requires much larger real numbers to record high percentage rates. What regions experienced the highest growth rates in real numbers, and what state became the most populous because of shifting residential trends? When did this state become number one in population, and how many people lived there?

MAP 27.2 *The Rise of the Sun Belt, 1940–1960*

Increase in population

- Over 50%
- 20%–50%
- 10%–20%
- Under 10%

Decrease in population
- Under 10%

o Major Sun Belt cities

ALASKA (1959) 75%

HAWAII (1959) 26%

WASH. 19%
OREGON 16%
IDAHO 13%
MONTANA 14%
NORTH DAKOTA 2%
SOUTH DAKOTA 4%
WYOMING 13%
NEBRASKA 6%
MINN. 14%
WIS. 15%
IOWA 5%
MICH. 22%
NEVADA 78%
UTAH 29%
COLORADO 32%
KANSAS 14%
ILL. 15%
IND. 18%
OHIO 22%
CALIF. 48%
ARIZONA 73%
NEW MEXICO 39%
OKLAHOMA 4%
MO. 9%
KY. 3%
W.V. –7%
VA. 19%
TENN. 8%
N.C. 12%
ARK. 6%
TEXAS 24%
LA. 21%
MISS. 1%
ALA. 6%
GA. 14%
S.C. 12%
FLA. 78%
VT. 3%
ME. 6%
N.H. 13%
MASS. 9%
R.I. 8%
N.Y. 13%
PA. 7%
CONN. 26%
N.J. 25%
DEL. 40%
MD. 32%
D.C. –4%

Los Angeles
San Diego
Phoenix
Tucson
Dallas
San Antonio
Houston
New Orleans
Atlanta
Miami

PACIFIC OCEAN
ATLANTIC OCEAN
CANADA
MEXICO
Gulf of Mexico

2. What stimulated the population boom in the Southwest? What role did the cold war play in this boom? What state in particular benefited from a burgeoning defense industry?

_____

_____

_____

_____

_____

_____

_____

_____

_____

_____

_____

_____

3. What role did African Americans play in the western population boom?

_____

_____

_____

_____

_____

_____

_____

_____

EXPLORING THE MAP

1. One of the effects of the population boom in California and other states was the rise of totally planned communities, such as Lakewood, California (see pages 1080–1081 in the textbook). Write a promotional flier extolling the virtues of Lakewood, focusing on housing, jobs, and access to shopping.

_____

_____

_____

_____

_____

_____

_____

_____

_____

_____

_____

_____

2. One of the problems with living in the Sun Belt is the intense heat in the summer. Many of the southwestern states are largely desert areas. What technological development that became a consumer item after World War II helped make residing in the Southwest during the summer more comfortable?

_____

_____

_____

NOTES

CHAPTER 28

A DECADE OF REBELLION AND REFORM
1960–1968

Introduction

The election of John F. Kennedy as president in 1960 initiated a decade of incredible activity and change. Using his inaugural speech to motivate public activism, Kennedy inspired young people, African Americans, other minorities, and women to work for reform and their rights. See *The American Promise,* page 1101.

READING THE MAP

1. How many states did John F. Kennedy and Richard Nixon carry, respectively, in the 1960 election? Did the candidate carrying the most states win the election? Who also ran, and how many states did he carry?

   _____

   _____

   _____

   _____

2. Examining the electoral votes in the states won by each candidate, determine why Kennedy won the election.

   _____

   _____

   _____

3. Look at the trends in states won, and consider what the outcome of the election might have been if Harry Byrd had not been a candidate.

   _____

   _____

   _____

   _____

   _____

CONNECTING TO THE CHAPTER

1. Kennedy and Nixon tried to improve their chances through their party platforms and vice presidential candidates. What were their respective party platforms, and what was the strategy behind the vice presidential choice of each candidate? Who benefited most from his strategies?

   _____

   _____

   _____

   _____

   _____

   _____

   _____

MAP 28.1   The Election of 1960

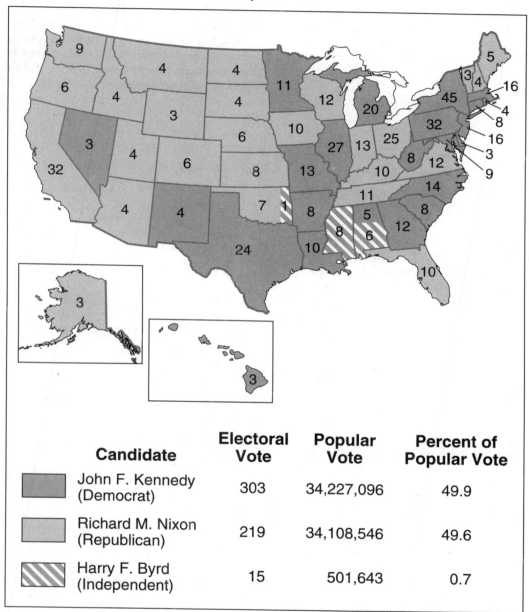

Candidate	Electoral Vote	Popular Vote	Percent of Popular Vote
John F. Kennedy (Democrat)	303	34,227,096	49.9
Richard M. Nixon (Republican)	219	34,108,546	49.6
Harry F. Byrd (Independent)	15	501,643	0.7

(Question 1 continues) _____

_____

_____

_____

_____

_____

_____

_____

_____

2. How did televised debates influence the outcome of the election? How did radio listeners and television watchers differ on the outcome of the debates?

_____

_____

_____

_____

_____

3. What role did television have on voter turnout?

_____

_____

_____

_____

EXPLORING THE MAP

1. John F. Kennedy's inaugural speech inspired a generation to greater social activism. Locate a copy of Kennedy's speech either on tape or in print. Do his words have the same power today as they did in 1960? Why, or why not?

_____

_____

_____

_____

_____

_____

_____

_____

_____

_____

_____

_____

_____

_____

_____

_____

NOTES

A DECADE OF REBELLION AND REFORM
1960–1968

Introduction

Though guaranteed the vote by the Fifteenth Amendment, African Americans in the South had been disfranchised. One of the major goals of the post–World War II civil rights movement was to recapture the voting rights southern blacks had lost at the turn of the century. See *The American Promise,* page 1118.

READING THE MAP

1. In the South generally, when did the biggest change in African American voter registration occur, and what was the magnitude of that change?

2. In each of the four periods shown in Map 28.2, which states had the highest and which had the lowest voter registration records?

3. Did any states record declines in African American voter registration between 1968 and 1976? If so, what states had the declines?

4. Since 1968, what is the average range of African American voter registration in the South?

CONNECTING TO THE CHAPTER

1. The power of African American voting was shown in the 1960 presidential election. What role did African American voters play in that election, and in what states was that role most evident?

MAP 28.2 *The Rise of the African American Vote, 1940–1976*

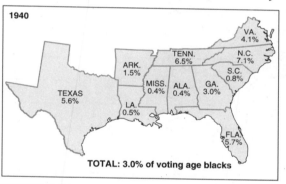

1940

VA. 4.1%
TENN. 6.5%
N.C. 7.1%
ARK. 1.5%
S.C. 0.8%
TEXAS 5.6%
MISS. 0.4%
ALA. 0.4%
GA. 3.0%
LA. 0.5%
FLA. 5.7%

TOTAL: 3.0% of voting age blacks

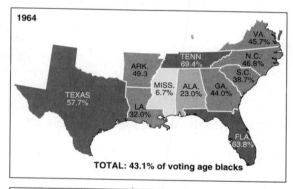

1964

VA. 45.7%
TENN. 69.4%
N.C. 46.8%
ARK. 49.3
S.C. 38.7%
TEXAS 57.7%
MISS. 6.7%
ALA. 23.0%
GA. 44.0%
LA. 32.0%
FLA. 63.8%

TOTAL: 43.1% of voting age blacks

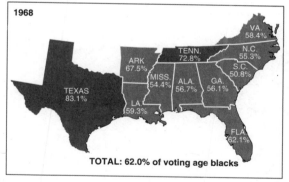

1968

VA. 58.4%
TENN. 72.8%
N.C. 55.3%
ARK 67.5%
S.C. 50.8%
TEXAS 83.1%
MISS. 54.4%
ALA. 56.7%
GA. 56.1%
LA. 59.3%
FLA. 62.1%

TOTAL: 62.0% of voting age blacks

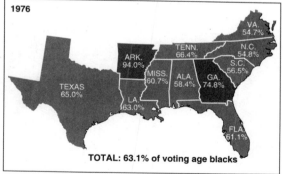

1976

VA. 54.7%
TENN. 66.4%
N.C. 54.8%
ARK. 94.0%
S.C. 56.5%
TEXAS 65.0%
MISS. 60.7%
ALA. 58.4%
GA. 74.8%
LA. 63.0%
FLA. 61.1%

TOTAL: 63.1% of voting age blacks

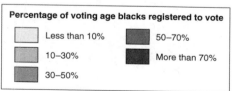

Percentage of voting age blacks registered to vote

Less than 10%
50–70%
10–30%
More than 70%
30–50%

2. The crusade to expand African American voting rights led to three major voting drives in the 1960s. What were these drives? When did they occur, and what were their targets? What organizations were involved? How were the voting rights supporters treated?

3. When was the Voting Rights Act passed?

EXPLORING THE MAP

1. The rise in African American voting had tremendous repercussions on the political culture of the United States. Write an essay that answers the question posed on page 1120–1121 of the textbook: What difference did black voting rights make?

NOTES

CHAPTER 29

VIETNAM AND THE LIMITS OF POWER
1961–1975

Introduction

The United States maintained a very active foreign policy in the Americas that often involved intervening in the affairs of many nations. See *The American Promise,* page 1139.

READING THE MAP

1. In what countries in Latin America and the Caribbean was the United States involved between 1954 and 1996? What countries avoided U.S. involvement?

    _____

    _____

    _____

    _____

    _____

2. One of the major aspects of U.S. involvement in Latin America and the Caribbean was the use of military forces. Complete the following chart to trace the deployment of U.S. troops. Use the boldface entry as a model. Then answer the question following the chart.

    Considering all the events listed in the chart, identify the primary reason or reasons for U.S. military intervention.

    _____

    _____

    _____

    _____

    _____

Date	Country	Event precipitating U.S. intervention
1964	**Panama**	**Anti-American rioting**
1965		
1983		
1989		
1994		

3. What Caribbean nation successfully resisted U.S. intervention?

_____

_____

_____

_____

CONNECTING TO THE CHAPTER

1. U.S. policy toward Latin America and the Caribbean changed over time. What was the major policy initiative aimed at improving relations with other American na-

tions? Who proposed this initiative? What was its goal? Was it successful? Why, or why not?

_____

_____

_____

_____

_____

_____

_____

MAP 29.1 U.S. Involvement in Latin America and the Caribbean, 1954–1996

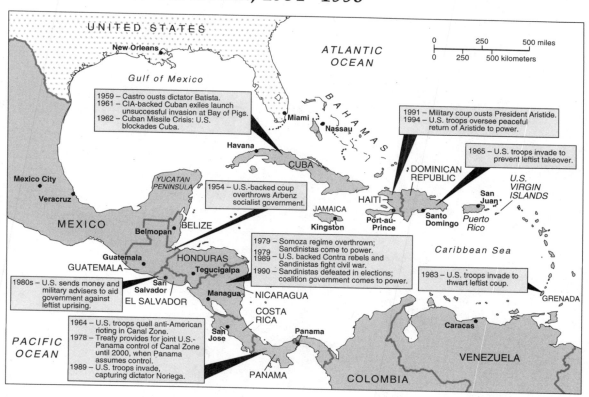

2. Cuba was the scene of two major actions. What were they? When did they occur? What happened, and what was the outcome of each action?

_____

_____

_____

_____

_____

_____

_____

_____

_____

_____

_____

_____

_____

EXPLORING THE MAP

1. Choose an example of U.S. involvement in the Caribbean, and draw two political cartoons about this episode, one supporting the actions from the side of the United States and the other criticizing it from the perspective of the other nation involved. You might portray moral, political, or democratic principles in your cartoons. Which cartoon best fits your opinion of this example of U.S. involvement in Latin America and the Caribbean?

NOTES

VIETNAM AND THE LIMITS OF POWER
1961–1975

Introduction

The Vietnam War was the nation's longest military conflict and the second time the United States intervened in an Asian nation. It also was the first international war that the United States lost. See *The American Promise*, page 1147.

READING THE MAP

1. What accord divided Vietnam into two nations? When was it signed, and where was the line of division drawn?

2. The Ho Chi Minh Trail, named for North Vietnam's leader, was a major supply line from North to South Vietnam. In what countries was the Trail located? What action did the United States take against the trail?

3. Hanoi and Saigon were the capitals of North and South Vietnam, respectively. What actions did the United States take against Hanoi, and what military acts did the North Vietnamese take against Saigon?

CONNECTING TO THE CHAPTER

1. The Gulf of Tonkin incident significantly expanded U.S. involvement in Vietnam. What was the incident? What was the extent of U.S. involvement before it occurred? How did the United States respond, and what was the extent of U.S. involvement after the incident?

MAP 29.2 *The Vietnam War, 1964–1975*

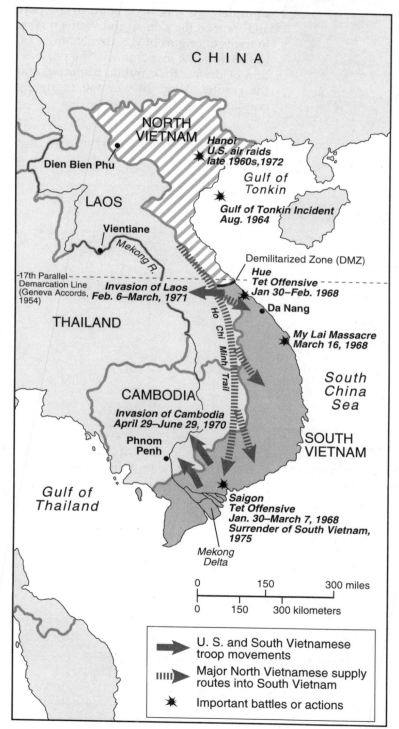

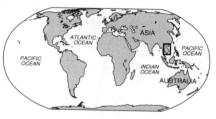

CHINA

NORTH
VIETNAM

Dien Bien Phu

Hanoi
*U.S. air raids
late 1960s, 1972*

*Gulf of
Tonkin*

LAOS

*Gulf of Tonkin Incident
Aug. 1964*

Vientiane

Mekong R.

Demilitarized Zone (DMZ)

17th Parallel
Demarcation Line
(Geneva Accords,
1954)

*Invasion of Laos
Feb. 6–March, 1971*

Hue
*Tet Offensive
Jan 30–Feb. 1968*

THAILAND

Ho Chi Minh Trail

Da Nang

*My Lai Massacre
March 16, 1968*

*South
China
Sea*

CAMBODIA

*Invasion of Cambodia
April 29–June 29, 1970*

**Phnom
Penh**

SOUTH
VIETNAM

*Gulf of
Thailand*

*Mekong
Delta*

Saigon
*Tet Offensive
Jan. 30–March 7, 1968
Surrender of South Vietnam,
1975*

| 0 | 150 | 300 miles |

| 0 | 150 | 300 kilometers |

➤ U. S. and South Vietnamese
troop movements

➤ Major North Vietnamese supply
routes into South Vietnam

✳ Important battles or actions

111

2. What was the Tet Offensive and how did it affect the war in Vietnam?

_____

_____

_____

_____

_____

_____

_____

3. What was the response in the United States to the invasion of Cambodia in 1970?

_____

_____

_____

_____

_____

_____

EXPLORING THE MAP

1. Complete the following chart to compare and contrast the Korean and Vietnam Wars in terms of origins of U.S. involvement, rationale for U.S. involvement, the prosecution of the conflict, public response, and the results. Then answer the following questions.

Which war, if either, do you think was justified? Why?

_____

_____

_____

_____

_____

_____

_____

_____

_____

_____

	Korean War	_Vietnam War_
Origins of U.S. involvement	**North Korean invasion of South Korea**	**Kennedy's foreign policy of aggressive anticommunism**
Rationale for U.S. involvement		
Prosecution of conflict		
Public response		
Results		

NOTES

CHAPTER 30

THE DECLINE OF TRUST AND CONFIDENCE

1968–1980

Introduction

The fight for women's rights did not end with the gaining of the vote in 1920. In the late 1960s and 1970s, the Equal Rights Amendment was a major focus of women's rights groups. See *The American Promise,* page 1184.

READING THE MAP

1. The ERA needed ratification by three-fourths of the states to become law. How many states ratified the amendment? How many were needed for passage? What states ratified and then rescinded their passage?

   _____

   _____

   _____

   _____

2. Were there are any regions that unanimously supported or opposed the ERA? If so, what were they? Where else was support for the ERA strong?

   _____

   _____

   _____

   _____

   _____

   _____

3. What action did your state take on the ERA?

   _____

   _____

CONNECTING TO THE CHAPTER

1. The struggle for the ERA was connected to a larger, long-standing women's rights movement. Who first proposed the ERA and when?

   _____

   _____

2. The ERA was part of a larger feminist movement. Who were the leaders of this movement? What organizations and publications were influential in the movement? What were their goals?

   _____

   _____

   _____

   _____

   _____

   _____

   _____

(Question 2 continues) _____

_____   _____

_____   _____

_____   _____

                                     _____

3. What was the goal of the ERA? When was   _____
   it passed by Congress? Who led the successful opposition, and what were their   _____
   main points of opposition?
                                               _____

_____   _____

_____   _____

_____   _____

_____   _____

MAP 30.1 *The Fight for the Equal Rights Amendment*

Legend:
- States that ratified the ERA
- States that did not ratify the ERA
- States that ratified and then rescinded ratification

EXPLORING THE MAP

1. Using the points of opposition to the ERA from question 3 in the previous section, write a short speech (two to three minutes) that either supports the opposition or attacks it. Give your speeches in class and then debate the ERA.

NOTES

THE DECLINE OF TRUST AND CONFIDENCE
1968–1980

Introduction

After World War II, the Middle East became a major trouble spot. A complex set of factors led to several wars and situations that sorely tested U.S. foreign policy in the region. See *The American Promise,* page 1192.

READING THE MAP

1. According to Map 30.2, which Middle Eastern nations did the United States become involved with?

   _____

   _____

   _____

   _____

2. OPEC stands for Organization of Petroleum Exporting Countries. Which Middle Eastern nations belonged to OPEC? What important resource did these nations possess?

   _____

   _____

   _____

   _____

3. What kinds of violent actions occurred in the Middle East?

   _____

   _____

   _____

   _____

   _____

   _____

   _____

CONNECTING TO THE CHAPTER

1. What were the cornerstones of U.S. foreign policy in the Middle East? Were they compatible? Why, or why not?

   _____

   _____

   _____

   _____

   _____

   _____

   _____

2. What precipitated the oil embargo in 1973 and how was it resolved?

_____

_____

_____

_____

_____

_____

_____

3. What was the U.S. policy toward Iran, and how did U.S. actions and that policy help precipitate the hostage crisis in 1979?

_____

_____

_____

_____

_____

_____

_____

MAP 30.2   *The Middle East, 1948–1996*

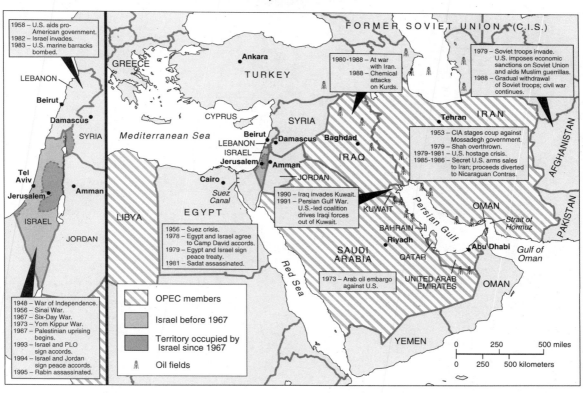

1958 – U.S. aids pro-American government.
1982 – Israel invades.
1983 – U.S. marine barracks bombed.

1980-1988 – At war with Iran.
1988 – Chemical attacks on Kurds.

1979 – Soviet troops invade. U.S. imposes economic sanctions on Soviet Union and aids Muslim guerrillas.
1988 – Gradual withdrawal of Soviet troops; civil war continues.

1953 – CIA stages coup against Mossadegh government.
1979 – Shah overthrown.
1979-1981 – U.S. hostage crisis.
1985-1986 – Secret U.S. arms sales to Iran; proceeds diverted to Nicaraguan Contras.

1990 – Iraq invades Kuwait.
1991 – Persian Gulf War. U.S.-led coalition drives Iraqi forces out of Kuwait.

1956 – Suez crisis.
1978 – Egypt and Israel agree to Camp David accords.
1979 – Egypt and Israel sign peace treaty.
1981 – Sadat assassinated.

1973 – Arab oil embargo against U.S.

1948 – War of Independence.
1956 – Sinai War.
1967 – Six-Day War.
1973 – Yom Kippur War.
1987 – Palestinian uprising begins.
1993 – Israel and PLO sign accords.
1994 – Israel and Jordan sign peace accords.
1995 – Rabin assassinated.

OPEC members
Israel before 1967
Territory occupied by Israel since 1967
Oil fields

4. What initiative was a breakthrough in seeking peace in the Middle East? Who was involved, and what were the provisions?

_____

_____

_____

_____

_____

_____

_____

_____

_____

_____

_____

_____

_____

_____

_____

_____

_____

_____

_____

_____

_____

_____

_____

_____

_____

_____

_____

_____

EXPLORING THE MAP

1. Using the provisions of the Camp David accords as a model, devise a proposal to gain the release of the U.S. hostages in Iran.

_____

_____

_____

_____

_____

_____

_____

_____

_____

_____

_____

_____

_____

_____

_____

_____

_____

_____

_____

_____

_____

_____

_____

_____

_____

_____

_____

_____

NOTES

CHAPTER 31

THE REAGAN-BUSH COUNTERREVOLUTION
1980–1991

Introduction

In a reverse irony of the domino theory, the Communist bloc in Eastern Europe, including the Soviet Union, collapsed in 1989 and 1990, creating an entirely new political situation as new nations and new governments emerged. See *The American Promise,* page 1248.

READING THE MAP

1. Create a timeline of the collapse of communism in Eastern Europe, leaving out the Soviet Union. Which country was the first to overthrow its Communist government? Which was the last? Which nations experienced violence?

   _____

   _____

   _____

   _____

   _____

   _____

   _____

   _____

   _____

2. In which nations did elections lead to the change in government?

   _____

   _____

   _____

3. When did the Soviet Union dissolve? What new nations emerged out of the dissolution? Which nations did not join the Commonwealth of Independent States?

   _____

   _____

   _____

   _____

   _____

   _____

CONNECTING TO THE CHAPTER

1. What Soviet leader began the movement that led to the collapse of the Soviet Union? What problems did he try to solve, and what were his two major initiatives?

   _____

   _____

   _____

   _____

(Question 1 continues) _____

_____

_____

_____

_____

_____

_____

_____

2. What policy launched by Ronald Reagan contributed to Soviet problems? Did it create any problems for the United States? If so, what problems?

_____

_____

_____

_____

_____

_____

MAP 31.2 Events in Eastern Europe, 1989–1992

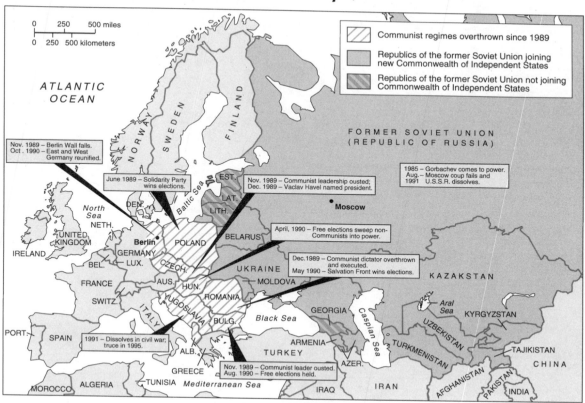

3. How did the collapse of communism change the role of the United States in Europe?

_____

_____

_____

_____

_____

_____

_____

_____

_____

_____

_____

_____

_____

_____

_____

_____

_____

_____

_____

_____

_____

_____

_____

_____

_____

_____

_____

_____

EXPLORING THE MAP

1. Besides Mikhail Gorbachev, Map 31.2 contains one name—Vaclav Havel. Research Havel's background and write a brief biography of him that not only describes his life but explains why he is important.

_____

_____

_____

_____

_____

_____

_____

_____

_____

_____

_____

_____

_____

_____

_____

_____

_____

_____

_____

_____

_____

_____

_____

_____

_____

NOTES

THE REAGAN-BUSH COUNTERREVOLUTION
1980–1991

Introduction

The invasion of Kuwait by Iraq provoked international condemnation culminating in the Gulf War in February 1991. See *The American Promise,* page 1249.

READING THE MAP

1. What gulf did the war take place around, and where is this gulf located? What nations shown on the map border on the gulf?

2. What important natural resource abounds in the gulf region?

3. From what country did the United States-led forces attack Iraq? What nations sent forces to fight against Iraq?

4. Some of the world's earliest civilizations, including the cultures considered the cradle of Western civilization, arose along two rivers in Iraq. What are these rivers?

CONNECTING TO THE CHAPTER

1. Who was the Iraqi leader who began the Gulf War? How did he justify the invasion of Kuwait? What other reasons were probably more important? What other actions besides invading Kuwait did Iraq take that intensified the situation?

MAP 31.3 *The Gulf War, February 1991*

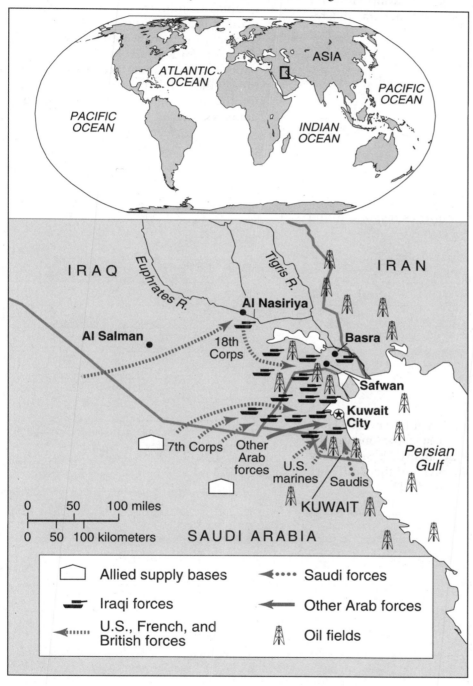

2. Before the war, how did President Bush respond to the invasion of Kuwait? How did
   he justify his response? What was this response called?

   _____

   _____

   _____

   _____

   _____

3. How did the Soviet Union, the United Nations, and other countries respond to the
   Iraqi invasion?

   _____

   _____

   _____

   _____

   _____

4. What was the invasion of Iraq called? How
   long did the air war last? How long did the
   land war last? How many U. S. military
   personnel were involved in the Gulf War?
   How many Americans died?

   _____

   _____

   _____

   _____

   _____

EXPLORING THE MAP

1. Chapter 31 indicates that many Americans
   wanted to delay military action to see if
   economic sanctions would force Iraqi withdrawal from Kuwait. Referring to newspaper and magazine accounts from the
   time of the Gulf War, write an essay weigh-
   ing the pros and cons of war versus economic sanctions.

   _____

   _____

   _____

   _____

   _____

   _____

   _____

   _____

   _____

   _____

   _____

   _____

   _____

   _____

   _____

   _____

NOTES

CHAPTER 32

THE CLINTON ADMINISTRATION AND THE SEARCH FOR A POPULAR CENTER
1992–1997

Introduction

The election of 1992 reversed twelve years of Republican presidencies as the Democrats captured the top office. But the election also indicated that the nation had changed greatly since the last Democratic president held office. See *The American Promise*, page 1257.

READING THE MAP

1. How many states did Bill Clinton and George Bush carry, respectively, in 1992? In which regions was each stronger? Where did the two candidates seem to divide the vote equally?

   _____

   _____

   _____

   _____

2. Third-party candidate Ross Perot did not gain any electoral votes, but he did get 18.9 percent of the popular vote. What effect did his candidacy have on the eventual totals for the popular vote?

   _____

   _____

   _____

3. Examine the electoral and popular vote totals and geographic spread of those voting for Clinton and for Bush. Do you think Bill Clinton did or did not win a national mandate? Or do the results make it impossible to say whether his mandate was national or not? Explain your answer.

   _____

   _____

   _____

   _____

   _____

   _____

CONNECTING TO THE CHAPTER

1. What was new about the Clinton–Gore ticket generally and in political philosophy compared with previous Democratic candidates?

   _____

   _____

   _____

   _____

   _____

   _____

MAP 32.1 The Election of 1992

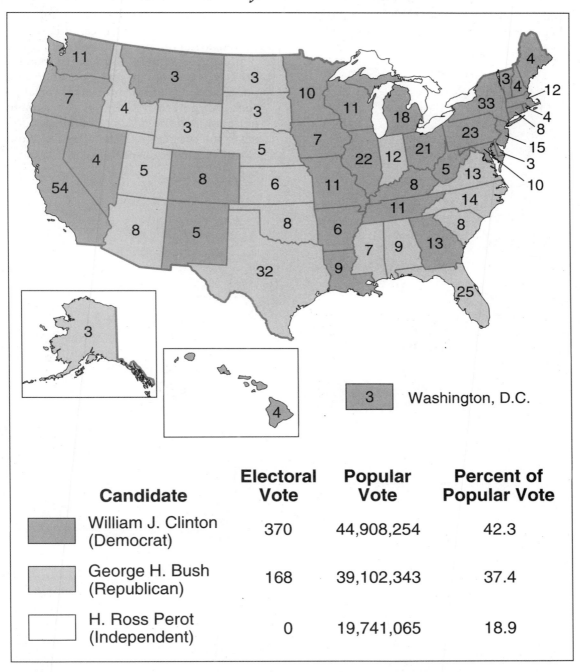

Candidate	Electoral Vote	Popular Vote	Percent of Popular Vote
William J. Clinton (Democrat)	370	44,908,254	42.3
George H. Bush (Republican)	168	39,102,343	37.4
H. Ross Perot (Independent)	0	19,741,065	18.9

2. What did Bush focus his campaign on, and what did Clinton stress? What was the public concerned about? Which candidate better addressed the concerns of the public?

_____

_____

_____

_____

_____

_____

_____

_____

3. What was the focus of Ross Perot's candidacy? Why did he prove so effective, and whom did his candidacy hurt more—Bush or Clinton?

_____

_____

_____

_____

_____

_____

_____

_____

_____

_____

_____

_____

_____

_____

EXPLORING THE MAP

1. In 1992, most voters desired change and new ideas, but none of the candidates presented a liberal program. Write a party platform for a liberal third party that addresses the concerns of the public and poses liberal solutions: focus on social issues, support for a strong government presence, and the needs of minorities. Refer to the programs of the New Deal and Great Society for ideas.

_____

_____

_____

_____

_____

_____

_____

_____

_____

_____

_____

_____

_____

_____

_____

_____

_____

_____

_____

NOTES

THE CLINTON ADMINISTRATION AND THE SEARCH FOR A POPULAR CENTER
1992–1997

Introduction

In 1996, Bill Clinton became the first Democratic president since Franklin D. Roosevelt to win reelection after a full first-term. Unlike Roosevelt, Clinton won during a period of general economic well-being. The 1996 election also was very similar to that of 1992. See *The American Promise*, page 1264.

READING THE MAP

1. As in 1992, the 1996 presidential election had three candidates. Two had run in 1992 —Clinton and Perot. How many states did Clinton carry? How many did Dole? How did the number of states carried by each compare with the Democratic and Republican totals in 1992? How did Perot do in 1996 compared with 1992?

   _____

   _____

2. Referring to Map 32.1 on the 1992 election, what states carried by Clinton in 1992 were won by Dole? What states won by Bush in 1992 went for Clinton in 1996?

   _____

   _____

   _____

3. Though Clinton carried one fewer state in 1996, his popular and electoral vote totals were larger than in 1992. Taking a look at the shift in states going from Republican to Democratic and vice versa between 1992 and 1996, determine whether the exchange benefited Clinton or Dole. What state that switched parties was most important, and why?

   _____

   _____

   _____

   _____

   _____

   _____

   _____

CONNECTING TO THE CHAPTER

1. What happened in the 1994 congressional election, and what did the results portend for the 1996 election?

   _____

   _____

   _____

   _____

MAP 32.2   The Election of 1996

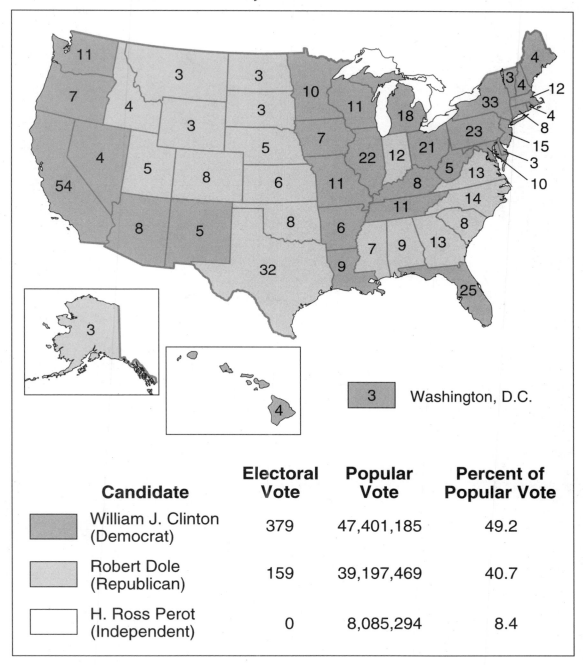

Candidate	Electoral Vote	Popular Vote	Percent of Popular Vote
William J. Clinton (Democrat)	379	47,401,185	49.2
Robert Dole (Republican)	159	39,197,469	40.7
H. Ross Perot (Independent)	0	8,085,294	8.4

2. What was President Clinton's status in 1994, and what did he do to change it by 1996?

_____

_____

_____

_____

_____

_____

_____

_____

_____

_____

_____

_____

_____

_____

_____

_____

3. What did the results of the presidential and congressional contests in 1996 tell about the public's opinion on the makeup of the federal government?

_____

_____

_____

_____

_____

_____

_____

_____

_____

_____

EXPLORING THE MAP

1. The 1996 election revealed a significant gender gap as 54 percent of women voted for Clinton compared with 38 percent for Dole. Referring to newspaper and magazine coverage of the election, identify the reasons why women preferred Clinton and draw a political cartoon that shows why Clinton appealed to women voters.